ONEGOOD
WORK AT A TIME

Simple Things You Can Do to Make a Difference

ONE GOOD
WORK AT A TIME

Frances Sheridan Goulart

SORIN BOOKS Notre Dame, Indiana

www.sorinbooks.com

ISBN-10 1-893732-90-8

ISBN-13 978-1-893732-90-2

Cover and text design by Katherine Robinson Coleman

Printed and bound in the United States of America.

Library of Congress Cataloging-in-Publication Data

Goulart, Frances Sheridan.

  The power of one : saving the world (and your soul) one good work at a time / Frances Sheridan Goulart.

     p. cm.

  ISBN-13: 978-1-893732-90-2 (pbk.)

  ISBN-10: 1-893732-90-8 (pbk.)

 1. Good works (Theology) I. Title.

  BT773.G68 2006

  234—dc22

                                          2005031757

DEDICATION

Dedicated to the people who
make my life a good work:

my family, Ron, Sean, and Steffan;

and my animal companions.

CONTENTS

INTRODUCTION

Trust in the LORD, and do good. . . .

❧ Psalm 37:3

Nobis es, (it's up to us), as the early Christians put it.

Doing God's work is an equal opportunity ministry to which we are all called. Yet, how often do we exempt ourselves from spiritual activism for a wide range of reasons—from insufficient time to insufficient funds? Insufficient will may be more to the point.

"What good is it, my brothers and sisters, if you say you have faith but do not have works?" we are asked in James 2:14–16. "Can faith save you? If a brother or sister is naked and lacks daily food, and one of you says to them, 'Go in peace; keep warm and eat your fill,' and yet you do not supply their bodily needs, what is the good of that?"

Opportunities to be God's hands, eyes, and ears in the world for the greater good are all around us, ready-made for the busiest schedule, suitable for the most constrained of budgets or the most limited of physical or social situations. The scriptures of all religions are filled with injunctions to do the right thing. "The shortest way to God is to bring compassion to the soul of your neighbor," wrote the Persian mystic Aby Saaid, who begged food for the poor long before the birth of Christ.

Similarly, Muhammad instructed us that God has mercy upon those who are merciful to others. And in our own tradition, in his letter to Titus (3:18), Paul mentions the importance of doing good, and loving what is good, seven times.

INTRODUCTION

As a bonus, service is self-serving. As physician Elaine R. Ferguson related in an article for *Spiritual Medicine* magazine,

> I decided to volunteer at a hospital shelter for babies born to women addicted to cocaine; I thought I would help the babies with my presence and medical expertise. After the first few weeks, however, I saw a change in the equation: who was doing the giving and who the receiving? I felt unconditional love and acceptance coming from the babies. They didn't care that I was a physician; they didn't know my name, who I was. Each responded to me in the most primal, immediate way: they received my loving attention and gave me back love.

Giving unconditional love because we were loved first by him who created us helps to restore our sense of belonging, our recognition that humankind is one big family.

The Power of ONE

Just reflect:

- ⊚ Could you spend fifteen minutes of your lunch hour twice a week speaking by phone to a lonely senior in your community?
- ⊚ Could you sacrifice an hour of television each week writing letters to local papers and elected officials advocating for the poor, the homeless, the hungry?
- ⊚ Could you computer-mentor an underachieving child with his or her homework once a week?
- ⊚ Could you stop off to read a blind person's mail to her once a week?
- ⊚ Could you join or organize a prayer circle to lift up the needs of people in your parish, the community, or the global community each day?

Those who love all . . . are the ones who so focus their lives that all they do is for the good of others.

Levels of Light, The Book of Mormon

INTRODUCTION

Good works come in the form of countless small-is-beautiful good turns as well as world class acts of altruism. You don't have to join the Peace Corps or a Peacemaker Team to be a power of one. You don't necessarily even have to get out of the easy chair or leave the computer to put your compassion into action. Doing your part as God's partner in acts of peace, love, and charity is a matter of making the Beatitudes a building block in your everyday life. In the words of global activist Robert Muller:

Decide to Network

Use every letter you write
Every conversation you have
Every meeting you attend
To express your fundamental beliefs and dreams
Affirm to others
The vision of the world you want
Network through thought
Network through action
Network through love
Network through the spirit
You are the center of a network

The Power of ONE

You are the center of the world
You are a free, immensely powerful source
of life and goodness
Affirm it
Spread it
Radiate it
Think day and night about it
And you will see a miracle happen
the greatness of your own life
In a world of big powers, media and
monopolies
But of six billion individuals
Networking is the new freedom
the new democracy
a new form of happiness

Some thoughts on how to affirm, spread, radiate, and live out your covenant as a walk-the-talk Christian each day follow in the pages ahead.

Nobis es.

Good Works in

PRAYER

Wired for Wednesday Prayer: Do you like to pray in community? Visit the Shalem Institute (www.shalem.org). Their mission is "to be an ecumenical community responding to a call to help mediate God's Spirit in the world." *Shalem* is Hebrew for wholeness. Scripture speaks of serving God with *lev shalem*, a whole heart. The Institute also offers spiritual direction, including a long-term Personal Spiritual Deepening Extension program.

A Sacred Space for Prayer: Have you ceased praying without ceasing? Recharge at Sacred Space (www.sacredspace.ie), a project of the Jesuit Community Center in Ireland. Sacred Space offers different ways to reflect and pray every day of the year (including a Lenten retreat and *Praying with the Pope*), with on-screen guidance and scripture in nineteen languages. Between the praise and the (spiritual) ammunition, keep on the path by reading the website's yearly prayer book *Sacred Space.* It can be purchased through publisher Ave Maria Press (www.avemariapress.com).

Passing the Peace: Do you have a favorite prayer for peace? Pass it on. Make multiple holy card-sized copies and place one in every letter you write, or bill you mail. You can also make it a permanent signature at the bottom of all your e-mails.

Power Praying for Peace: Would you like to join a community promoting universal prayer on a daily basis? Visit www.prayforpeace.com and receive a peace prayer via e-mail twice daily to pray with others around the globe.

Sacred 24/7: Make matters of the spirit a matter of course each day. Pray with your life—performing each of the day's activities with purpose and intention, taking the time to move mindfully through the activity—from driving to work to arranging a vase of flowers. Make each activity an offering back to your source. You may wish to create a mantra to say before starting a project—as simple as one word or two—*Spiritus Sanctus, Come Jesus,* or *Breath of God Breathe on Me.*

Where There Are Two Gathered: Lonely? Become a prayer partner, joining the fellowship of the faithful worldwide who are petitioning, praising, or uniting their spirits to the Creator. Become a prayer partner at the Urban Rescue Mission (www.urm.com), one of the largest rescue missions in the U.S., where staff, guests, and volunteers join hands daily, literally or digitally, to pray for every homeless person who passes through their doors. As a member of the fellowship, you will receive a list of prayer requests once a month via e-mail.

The non-doing of any evil; the performance of what is helpful; the cleansing of one's mind, This is the teaching of the Awakened.

Buddhavagga (Buddhist Pali scripture)

A New Q & A: What does twenty-first century Christianity look (and sound) like? Hear and see a sample at Living the Questions (www.living thequestions.com). The twelve week Living the Questions DVD and web-based small group study course proposes a revolutionary re-visioning of Christianity and includes author-speakers John Cobb, John Shelby Spong, and Marcus Borg as well as re-interpretations of theological ideas and jazz versions of traditional hymns. Unlike more traditional courses like the Alpha curriculum, Living the Questions studies the questions rather than just presenting answers.

For Bible Bibliophiles: Are you looking for the Good Book for computer-age Christians? Consider the Franklin Electronic Bible—King

James, New International version, or choose an electronic bible with both. Nearly pocket-sized, it locates any biblical reference or passage in an instant. You can also try the Holman Bible Dictionary and the PDA-sized Exhaustive Concordance of the Bible. Details at www.franklin.com.

Tough Love Devotions: "Love your enemies" we are urged in Matthew 5:44. But it's not easy to pray for our enemies, or at least those with whom you have a quarrel or find difficult, distasteful, or repellant politically, spiritually, or philosophically. Start small (a neighbor, a distant relative) and work up to the head of the political party you disagree with, a political dictator, a racist organization like the Ku Klux Klan, or the CEO of an exploitative multinational corporation. Choose one each week and stop daily to pray that he/she/it will be reconciled to God's grace.

Pray and Prosper: Recent demographic studies indicate that church-going correlates with increased life expectancy and lower blood pressure. After

services, eat lightly at coffee hour. The Japanese and French who consume smaller portions and eat less often enjoy a longer life-span than big-meal, multi-meal Americans.

Mea Culpa: A good way to come clean spiritually is to confess your sins and be reconciled. Make it a regular practice to go to confession, if that is part of your tradition; or, create your own sacred ritual at the end of each day or week. Take the time to review your failings, re-state your intentions, and make a profession of contrition in any way you find appropriate. Take enough time to make it meaningful.

Soulful Wakeup Calls: Wake up and be awakened. After you've read the morning's scripture, add a little Zen. You can sign up for e-mailed reflections from Zen masters at Daily Zen (www.dailyzen.com).

Good Works in the
HOME

Cheers: "The best way to cheer yourself up," wrote Mark Twain, "is to cheer somebody else up." And you don't even have to become a leave-home volunteer. Start small. Practice smiling (use a mirror) and pass it on everywhere you go, everywhere you are (start at home). You'll feel the warmth and so will everyone you meet. And as a bonus, your body will respond by lowering stress hormones and strengthening your immune system.

Time Trip: When we kill time, says Buddhist Lama Surya Das (author of *Awakening the Buddha Within*) we deaden ourselves. A better way to handle time is to use it for "things that quicken the sprit" says Das. Taking a short trip? Use the free time for meditation or journaling. On a long trip get out of your comfort zone and quicken your spirit with a book by someone with a different spiritual or political viewpoint than yours. Open your mind and heart and look for common ground.

Make Days Holy: Do you have your own personal holy days? Commemorate happy occasions, but also sad or life-changing events. Attending to these markers may bless you with insights into the richness of the experience or help you to grieve losses in a new way. Begin by commemorating the death of a partner, parent, child, or friend on one day a year. Light candles and spend time alone or spend an hour in waking meditation outdoors. Take a trip to a favorite place, or engage in a loved activity of the deceased to honor his/her spirit. Just as the rituals of secular and religious holidays can provide comfort and give form to our lives, so can private holy days.

Self Cherishing: Your body is a temple. Honor it by feeding it responsibly and imaginatively. Switch to plant-based meals that build your health and that of your family, spare the lives of animals, honor the environment, and give back to Mother Earth. For starter meal ideas and recipes, visit EarthSave International (www.earth save.org), The Vegetarian Resource Group (www.vrg.org), or VegSource (www.vegsource .com).

Bell, Book, and Zafu: Is today Ramadan, Sukkot, or St. Francis's feast day? You'll know if you start your calendar day with a glance at a religious planning calendar. The Christian Planning Calendar (from Morehouse Publishing, http://morehousegroup.com) cites all religious observances and seasons for Protestant, Anglican, Roman Catholic, Orthodox, Islamic, and Jewish faiths, as well as secular holidays. And once it's on the wall, think ahead about one good work a day you'd like to do and write it in to make it official.

All the Other News: Start the day with the social justice news. Flip through the pages of the online newsletter *Salt of the Earth* (www.claretianpubs .org). Sponsored by the Claretians—a Roman Catholic community of priests, brothers, and lay men and women of all ages—*Salt of the Earth* covers news of social legislation, hunger, unemployment, and events affecting immigrants, and the marginalized of our society. There is also Stats, an online member exchange and an excellent self-help resource, with answers to any question imaginable in the social justice area.

Journaling with Jacob: Give your children a Genesis-inspired gift that keeps on giving. Jacob gathered his twelve sons before his death, Genesis tells us, to impart the wisdom of a lifetime. You can too, and you don't have to wait until last rites. Create an "Ethical Will," a non-legal document that imparts beliefs, life lessons, hopes, and wishes for your children and grandchildren. You can put them in writing, make an audio recording, or get another family member to videotape you telling your life story. (Make a copy for each child.) For more tips, read *Ethical Wills: Putting Your Values on Paper* by Barry K. Baines.

Spare Change Agents: Twenty-three million Americans go to bed hungry each night. For kids, this can mean stunted growth, learning disabilities, and depressed immunity. Add this reflection to grace at family meals and remind your kids to help themselves to only what they can eat. Keep a "Hunger Piggy" bank on the table, encouraging everyone to add whatever spare change they have at the end of the day. Once a month, turn the contents over to a local food shelter.

Tea Twice: Get inner and outer health from a single teabag. Try an antioxidant rich herbal tea like Rooibos of White Tea, then squeeze out the bag and place it on your eyelids at the end of a busy day, after work, or before prayer.

Beach Bible: Best book for the beach this summer? How about the Bible, plus an easy guide to the good book? *A Newcomer's Guide to the Bible* focuses on themes and timelines in both the Old and New Testaments and helps you read the Bible in a new and deeper way. *A Newcomer's Guide to the Bible* can be found through College Press Publishing (www.college press.com).

Holy Curiosity: If you're curious about something Judaic, go to the site of *Tikkun* magazine (www.tikkun.org) and Ask the Rabbi, editor Rabbi Michael Lerner. No questions? Get a taste of Lerner's own holy curiosity by reading his editorials, or his books, which include *Spirit Matters: Global Healing and the Wisdom of the Soul* and *Jewish Renewal: A Path to Healing and Transformation. Tikkun* is devoted to the pursuit of social justice, ecological sanity, and world peace. Sign up for one of their task forces or local committees and join the pursuit.

Peace Bonds: Buy a birthday, graduation, or thank you gift that keeps giving . . . life. Ten dollars will buy a Peace Bond, which in turn supports the creation of an international Nonviolent Peaceforce trained for nonviolent intervention throughout the world. To learn more and to order bonds, visit Nonviolent Peaceforce (www.nonviolentpeaceforce.org).

Big Apple: Bring the apples of your eye face-to-face with God's little green and red apples. Look for a local orchard or farm where you can spend

the afternoon picking apples. As a bonus, you can treat your kids to fresh cider, pie, and donuts on site. Type "apple picking" and your location into any search engine to get started.

Taste and Tithe: Migrant farm workers help feed the nation, but who feeds the workers? The typical migrant farm family earns less than $23,000 (below the poverty level). Few workers have health insurance, even though they are often exposed to highly toxic farming chemicals. As a family, vote to give up dessert, wine, or soda once a week and send the monies saved to the Harvest of Hope Foundation (www.harvest ofhope.net). Funds are used for health, medical expenses, and education.

Lit Kids: More than half of all low-income families have no children's books in their homes. First Book, a national children's literacy organization is working to change that, one read at a time. Next time you book shop for your children at Amazon online or at Barnes and Noble around the corner, buy one for a bookless kid too, or set aside the amount you just spent to send to First Book (www.firstbook.org).

Fire Your Anger: Got anger? Think nature. Use a totem from nature to transform your negative moods. Instead of raising your voice or your fist, close your eyes and imagine your anger as a bird, animal, waterwheel, or fire and let it take off. Picture your angry feelings as a giant wave, rising to a crescendo then crashing into the sea of God's love. Or, picture your anger as a fire with flames growing higher and higher until they reach the extinguishing hand of God. For homework, read *Anger: Wisdom for Healing the Flames* by Thich Nhat Hahn.

Self Help for the Hungry: "Give me the strength never to disown the poor," wrote Hindu teacher Rabindranath Tagore. Keep that reminder next to the take-out menus in your kitchen, along with the address of Freedom from Hunger (www.freefromhunger.org). Their mission is to help families fight poverty with hope and dignity. Freedom from Hunger targets women who earn $1 a day or less in the developing world, offering them tools such as micro loans and life skills that lead to self reliance. Skip the takeout one night a month and help a hungry family feed its children for a week.

Unconditional Love: "It is not just a matter of what we accomplish outwardly in the world but of what we give humanity in every situation," said Albert Schweitzer. The best thing we can give is unconditional love, everyday, to every person we meet, in every situation, letting everyone we meet see Christ in us. To keep you on message, hang the For Peace and Justice calendar from Fellowship of Reconciliation on your wall (www.forusa.org).

Holistic Half-Pints: Demonstrate earth stewardship when you send your children off to school by:

- Choosing containers that don't leach toxins into food or drink, specifically Plastics #3, #6, and #7.

- Looking for petrochemical-free biodegradable cutlery, cups, food containers, and storage bags made from recycled paper, corn or potato starch or sustainably harvested trees.

- Packing their lunches in reusable non-leaching stainless steel thermoses and metal lunch pails.

- Buying them recycled cardboard pens or biodegradable pens.

- Choosing recycled chlorine-free paper.

Go to Green Earth Office Supply (www.green earthofficesupply.com) for anything you can't locate at Staples or Office Depot. For more information go to the Paper Product Report at The Green Guide (www.thegreenguide.com).

For the Birds: Is your house a home to the birds? Put up feeders, birdhouses, and nesting boxes in your backyard. Or attract hummingbirds with a special hummingbird feeder. Get acquainted with the bird life in your yard by joining the local branch of the National Audubon Society (www.audubon.org) or a nearby nature discovery center.

Beyond the To-Do List: Between brushing your teeth and closing your eyes for the night, practice reconciliation. Sit and reflect at day's end, review the day's events, your attitude, the quality of your interactions with others. Did you express unconditional love? Did you walk in Christ? Note the work to be done and pray for forgiveness and discernment. Perhaps light a candle, listen to your favorite hymn, chant, psalm, or observe five minutes of do-nothing silence. Experiment until you've created a meaningful ritual that will help you bring closure to the last twenty-four hours and peace to the next.

Spiritual Greetings: Forget secular greetings. Sacralize that special day with a Christian e-card from St. Anthony Messenger Press (www.catholicgreetings.org). Special themes include pet blessings, World Peace day, and your favorite saint's feast day.

Svadhyaya and Cinema: The yogic practice of *svadhyaya* calls us to look for inspirational scripture and readings to use as resources for contemplation of self and to rest in the practice of *japa mantra*, repetition of your chosen mantra for ten to twenty minutes daily. To support your spirit when you're not meditating, join the Spiritual Cinema Circle (www.spiritual cinemacircle.com) for films that open the heart. The Spiritual Cinema Circle offers DVDs that will "warm your heart and stir your soul."

Prayers and Pears: Are your meals the meditative experiences they were meant to be? They can be if you remember that food reveals our connection to God's earth. Buddhist monk and author Thich Nhat Hanh recommends breathing deeply, smiling at our table companions, and using this prayer:

> With the first taste, I promise to offer joy.

> With the second, I promise to help in relieving the suffering of others.

> With the third, I promise to see others' joy as my own.

> With the fourth I promise to learn the way of nonattachment and equanimity.

Keep a copy next to the salt and pepper shakers.

Freedom Fighter: "Only those who are attached to God alone are truly free" said the woman known as Peace Pilgrim. Become your own freedom fighter. Once a week select one aspect of your material life—things, places, people—and reflect on how you might loosen your attachment. For example, are there clothes and shoes in your closet that have not been used or worn for a year? Books you've read and will never open again? Furniture sitting in the basement? Take them to church for the next bazaar or tag sale or share your bounty with the local Salvation Army or Good Will. For more inspiration, visit the Peace Pilgrim website (http://peacepilgrim.org).

Spiritual Literacy: What are the year's best spiritual reads and how many of them are on your night table? Go to *Spirituality and Health* magazine's (www.spiritualityhealth.com) May/June 2005 issue to see The Best Spiritual Books of 2004 list. More on sacred reading can be found in *Spiritual Literacy: Reading the Sacred in Everyday Life* by Mary Ann Brussat and Frederic Brussat, contributing editors to the magazine, or try *Walking a Literary Labyrinth: A Spirituality of Reading* by Nancy M. Malone.

Browse with Purpose: Have a good Christian read online. Click up the social justice publication of the Claretians, *Salt of the Earth* (http://salt.claretianpubs.org) for a daily compilation of important religious happenings around the world.

The Jesus Attitude: "Your attitude should be the same as that of Christ Jesus," Paul instructed (Philippians 2:5 NKJ). Jesus never did anything without doing unto others. How about you? You can improve your family's health and someone else's wealth, by buying homegrown crops produced by previously homeless men and women. Look for groups like Houston's Urban Harvest, which operates almost fifty inner-city gardens. Even better, if you garden, set aside some of your bounty for the local soup kitchen. Learn about Plant a Row for the Hungry at www.gardenwriters.org/par.

God Talk: Research shows that prayer and meditation rebalance brain chemistry. Keep that talk interesting. Take your favorite prayers and cut them up so that each word is a separate square. Mix the squares and each day select one word to use as lectio divina (introspective meditation) and to center and bring you into stillness before your day begins. At the end of the month, assemble a new prayer out of the words selected. Alternately, each day create a new prayer with the shuffled words.

Board against Boredom: Inspire your kids by exposing them to world and local news. Clip human interest stories, calendar announcements of volunteer activities, or articles about a global problem or social issue and post on the family bulletin board, refrigerator, or drop them into your child's lunch box. Encourage them to read and share their reactions with you.

To give to others and be totally kind, this is the constant duty of the good.

Mahabharata (c. 800 BC)

Free Faith: Don't have time or money for a college course or retreat to deepen your faith? Do it free online. Go to www.spiritualityhealth.com (home of the magazine *Spirituality and Health*) and sign up for one of their e-courses which include Practicing Spirituality with Anglicans, Practicing Spirituality with Buddhists, and Practicing Spirituality in Nature. There are readings and lessons to read each day for four to six weeks.

Wrong with Dante: "I'd rather be wrong with Dante and Shakespeare and Milton, with Augustine of Hippo and Francis of Assisi, with Dr Johnson, Blake and Dostoyevsky than right with Voltaire, Rousseau, the Huxleys, Herbert Spencer, H. G. Wells and Bernard Shaw," said atheist-turned-Christian Malcolm Muggeridge, speaking of belief in God. Is what and who *you're* reading affirming your deepest beliefs? How did Shakespeare experience and express his God Hunger? How long has it been since you read Dante or Blake? Give up television or the Internet for a night and read a chapter of uplifting literature—fiction, poetry, biography, or autobiography.

Gratitude Attitude: "Giving thanks" routinely can help your children develop a greater appreciation for the necessities that they may take for granted—housing, clothing, food, family. Each night before dinner, say grace, encouraging your children to give thanks for something in their life. Add your own petition based on some current world event that calls for God's grace or mercy. This moment of reflection at dinnertime can make them more aware of the needs of others who must go without.

Divine Light, Leafy Green: We turn to divine light, say Buddhists, because of a natural spiritual tropism. To mirror and reinforce that turning, green your worship space, adding plants and keeping at least one vase of flowers that reflect the season. Choose a spot that receives divine light when you pray.

Wise Words: "The art of being wise is the art of knowing what to overlook" said William James. Practicing simplicity in all aspects of your life can help you to discern what's important versus what can be ignored. Two inexpensive primers to put you on the path: *Keeping Life Simple* and *Keeping Work Simple,* both by Karen Levine.

I Promise, I Promise: Make one change a month, big or small, for the next year that makes a difference in your spiritual, social, or physical life or the life of your family, friends, or in God's world at large. Pencil the changes into your wall calendar and your personal calendar in January to give you an upward and onward road map for the year ahead. Start with an environmental good deed for January, like switching to organic cotton. Cotton accounts for 25 percent of worldwide insecticide use and at least 107 of pesticides' active ingredients are carcinogenic (putting children most at risk). Organic cotton is not only better for the environment, it is economically smarter, since conventional cotton prices do not reflect the hidden costs paid by taxpayers such as billions of dollars in annual subsidies, hazardous waste disposal, and eco-damage. Get the whole story at www.sustainablecotton.org. An easy eco-deed: Stop using disposable cameras and return the ones you (or family and friends) have not used to the manufacturer for a small rebate.

From Gossip to God: Love God with all your heart, mind, and soul, urged Jesus. That leaves no room for gossip. Studies show that negative words come back to hurt the reputation (and conscience) of the gossiper rather than the victim. When you feel the urge to speak unkindly of another, look within and practice three minutes of silence, five minutes of journaling, or both. If you need more help moving from gossip to God, read *Gossip: Ten Pathways to Eliminate It from Your Life and Transform Your Soul* by Lori Palatnik.

Saved by Grace: "If you bring forth what is within you," says Jesus in the Gnostic Gospel of Thomas, "what you have will save you." What are those God-given talents, graces, and blessings? Are you using them in a way that will save you? Save one day a month to look at your saving graces from a larger perspective. List your life goals, your life purpose, reflect on your life mission at this moment. Are you living consciously on a path guided by your conscience in the lift of God's gifts? What do you need to change, tweak, begin again?

Got Prayer Block?: Get inspired daily. Subscribe to Upper Room (www.upperroom.org), Day by Day (www.forwardmovement.org), or the Daily Word (www.unityonline.org). Each devotional guide gives scripture readings and reflections for each day of the month. You also have the option of reading and reflecting online if your amen corner is in front of your PC.

Gingerbread Friend: There's no better way to express TLC to the family, friends, neighbors, and service people in your life than with homemade cookies. Set aside some time every week to bake a few batches of your favorite cookies. Try a new recipe each month. And, make an extra batch for the local nursing home or soup kitchen. For recipe ideas, go to AllRecipes (http://cookie.all recipes.com).

Earth Meditation: If you don't do seated meditation, how about kneeling and digging to find bliss? You could find more time for God if you spent less time mowing your lawn. Instead, plant a meadow of wildflowers. Pick a patch of your lawn and scatter a selection of colorful seeds and watch them sprout into a carpet of maintenance-free blooms. It'll be so inviting, you might want to move your meditation mat or prayer rug nearby.

Practice Silence: Without silence, the inward stillness in which God educates and molds us is impossible, said mystic Evelyn Underhill. See for yourself. Take a five minute silence break three times a day and take the *Friends of Silence* newsletter with you to read when you're through. Nan Merrill, the author/editor of *Friends of Silence* chooses a different focus each month— love, prayer, forgiveness, suffering, joy—and expresses it through the words of various authors, poets, and spiritual leaders. A donation of any amount will bring this spiritual nourishment to your mailbox monthly. Write Friends of Silence, 129 Skunk Hollow Rd, Jericho, VT 05465.

Sacred Cash: The bible contains 500 verses about prayer, 500 about faith and more than 2,000 about money. Examine your relationship with the not-so-almighty dollar. Does it come between you and your spiritual life? Find out and find new ways of using, not misusing your personal funds by reading *Your Money or Your Life* by Joe Dominguez and Vicki Robins, *Money as Sacrament: Finding the Sacred in Money* by Adele Azar-Rucquoi, or *A Woman's Book of Money and Spiritual Vision* by Rosemary Williams and Joanne Kabak.

Prayer Burn-out?: Before you get down on your knees, get a copy of Benedictine Sister Joan Chittister's *Life Ablaze: A Woman's Novena*, which offers biographies, lessons, intercessions, and prayers from such spiritual celebrities as Teresa of Avila, Dorothy Day, and Mary Magdalene.

Hesychast How-To: How we interact with the people in our lives, whether we are centers of peace or oases of compassion, makes a difference, says Archbishop Desmond Tutu. "The sum total of these interactions determines nothing less than the nature of human life on this planet." A Hesychast practice can help. Hesychast is the mystical tradition within the Eastern Orthodox Church in which you meditate with head bowed to focus on the heart center of your being. Empty your mind and repeat the Jesus Prayer (*Jesus Christ, Son of the living God, have mercy on me a sinner*) for a set period of time daily. Practitioners say that, like chanting, Hesychast can unite the pray-er with God and the Divine Light. Take a Hesychast break at high noon daily for a month and see if they're right.

Cultivate the Miracle of Life:  "To see a world in a grain of sand, and heaven in a wild flower, hold infinity in the palm of your hand and eternity in an hour," wrote the poet William Blake. Start today to glorify God. Cultivate a wildflower bed, or start an herb plant outdoors or in a windowsill pot, and watch the miracle of life unfold each day. Be God's partner in this bit of creation.

Kids against Pollution: Forget those after-school computer games; pick up that garden rake. Turn your kids into agents of environmental change. Introduce them to Kids Against Pollution (www.kidsagainstpollution.org), which works to empower kids in projects that educate about pollution while creating community gardens, setting up recycling centers, doing urban and shore cleanups, and sponsoring an annual Hike for a Planet and The World Summit on Sustainable Development that links kids worldwide.

A Different Happy Hour: Give thanks for healthy wholesome kids by helping those who aren't. Set aside an in-home "Happy Hour" once a month for local teens (with pop and snacks) and join the fight against underage drinking and driving. Did you know that underage drinkers consume as much as 20 percent of the alcohol consumed in the U.S.? Get involved with Mothers Against Drunk Driving (MADD) as a family, by distributing MADD's red ribbons wherever you go (www.MADD.org).

Alternative Birthday Gifts: What would you rather have for your birthday? A new tie or shawl, or a part in making literacy a reality for indigenous women and girls of Guatemala, where 94 percent are impoverished and 40 percent can't read? Fifty dollars will buy a year's worth of basic educational materials and pay for schooling for two Guatemalan young women. For details about these and other gifts (from eye care for Cambodians to Native American water rights and access to clean water) visit the Seva foundation (www.seva.org).

Extended Family Dinner: Cooking dinner for two or four? Think big and make that dinner for twelve (get the whole family to help you). You can package the extra servings and take them to the local soup kitchen. Call in advance to learn their needs and coordinate delivery time. Chef-impaired? Turn up to serve, wash dishes, or be a meal-time host.

Practice Peace: The practice of generosity can be considered karma yoga if it's performed with the intention of relieving suffering, as is the Prison Project of the Buddhist Peace Fellowship which helps prisoners use jail time to explore their spiritual natures. This includes ministry and correspondence between advocates and inmates to help them cope with the everyday violence behind bars. Members (you don't have to be a Buddhist to join) also work to counter violence to the environment, relieve the suffering of refugees, fight poverty, and speak up for economic justice. For more information or to join one of the more than fifty chapters (only $20 for students, seniors, and low-income beings practicing compassion), visit the Buddhist Peace Fellowship website (www.bpf.org).

Remember those who are in prison, as though you were in prison with them; those who are being tortured, as though you yourselves were being tortured.

Hebrews 13:3

Be Like Christ: Are you an incarnational Christian? According to the young adults of the Word Made Flesh mission project, that means being more Christian, being more like Christ who became one of us, who blessed the marginalized but spurned the hypocrites; and who lived and ate and walked among us, lifting up the downtrodden. To be uplifted by the work and words of Word Made Flesh, go towww.word madeflesh.com.

Better Living through Rules: Deepen your spiritual life by following a Rule of Life. In the third century, Christian monasteries wrote rules covering all aspects of life to keep God at their individual and collective center. The Rule of St. Benedict is among the best known today, but there are hundreds more. Living a rule of life can help you to be open to God in all aspects of your daily life. To learn more about customizing your own rule, read *Living Faith Day by Day: How the Sacred Rules of Monastic Traditions Can Help You Live Spiritually in the Modern World* by Debra K. Farrington, or visit Spirituality and Health (www.spiritualityhealth.com) and search for the e-course "Balancing Life by the Rule."

Blessing with Blooms: Friendship is priceless. Say so with flowers. Send a bouquet of flowers to a good friend, family member, or clergy person for no reason other than to acknowledge that special other in your life.

Your Patron Saint and Beyond: Be inspired each day before coffee. Keep a book of saints' feast days on your breakfast table and check it out each morning. Reflect on the special virtue this individual's life exhibits and see what opportunities arise for you to model this virtue in your own life over the next twenty-four hours.

Tapori Tykes: Would you rather enlist your child or godchild in the world peace movement than in the Cub or Eagle Scouts? Introduce kids to Tapori, a worldwide multicultural network of children aged seven to thirteen whose motto is "We want all children to have the same chance" (www.tapori.org). The name Tapori was chosen by the late Joseph Wresinski as a sign of solidarity with the poor children of India (taporis) who live in train stations caring for one another. He wrote to other children of the world, "You are like

Taporis when you look out for others. You can find ways to make the world a better place."

Mary, Margaret, and Josephine: Jesus was a man, but the New Testament would have been a different document without the courage and spirit of women like Mary, Margaret, Mary Magdalene, Pricilla, Phoebe, and others. How many women's stories do you know? Buy yourself a copy of *Great Women of the Bible in Art and Literature* by Dorothee Solle and Joe H. Kirchberger, and visit the New Testament Gateway's Women and Gender website (www.ntgateway.com/women) to learn more.

. . . **Love your neighbor as yourself.**

Romans 13:9

Good Works in the

WORKPLACE

The Golden Rules: Nothing is as universal as the "do unto others" ethic. Before you start your work day, go to the Temple of Understanding website (www.templeofunderstanding.org) and read the golden rules of eleven different faith traditions(www.templeofunderstanding.org/new Site/interfaithResources/goldenRules.php). Make a copy and keep it inside a desk drawer or on your blotter. Start each day by reading one rule and living your day in its light. For example, follow the Buddhist golden rule: "Hurt not others in ways that you yourself would find hurtful" (Udana Varga, 5:18).

Philanthropic Phone Call: Sign up for Working Assets phone service (www.workingassets .com) and 1 percent of your local and long distance charges will be donated to nonprofit groups like International Medical Corps, National Coalition for the Homeless, and the American Civil Liberties Union. In 2004, Working Assets donated almost seven million dollars to the nonprofits it represents.

Be constant in prayer and give alms and what good you have sent before you, so will you find it with God.

Qur'an (c. 625)

The Shirt on Your Back: If you're not in the workplace anymore but your closets are filled with suits and dress shoes, donate them to Dress for Success (www.dressforsuccess.org) to clothe a low income woman entering the workplace. Or, help a high school girl go to the prom by getting your (or your daughter's) old prom gown (and/or accessories) out of storage and sending it to The Glass Slipper Project (www.glassslipperproject.org).

Being Christ-bearers: Be uplifted and inspired ten times a year at lunch. Subscribe to *Christopher News Notes* (www.christophers.org), a newsletter that delivers ten times a year from the Christophers. The Christophers' goal is to be Christ-bearers, bringing his light into the world. The Christophers encourage personal responsibility for raising the standards of all phases of human endeavor. Topics covered in the *News Notes* include *It's a Mad Mad World* (how to get a handle on anger and rage) and *The Changing Workplace* (the relationship between what we do for a living and who we are).

Lights On: "When we look for the light of God in people, an incredible thing happens. We find it more and more in people," says Archbishop Desmond Tutu. Let this "looking" be your spiritual practice at work today. See this light in the people you encounter everyday; those whose images you see on TV, over the radio, or via phone; even those you meet through their words in books and periodicals. Do not judge them, but bless them and then bless yourself, creating a bond between Christ and his creatures. Visit the Desmond Tutu Peace Centre online (www.tutu.org) to help nurture peace in your self and your world.

Jobs and Justice: What is the best way to give thanks for the job you have or to join the fight for justice in job hiring for others? Visit the Jobs with Justice website (www.jwj.org). Read all about the fight for job security and the right to organize and strike. Local coalitions across the country provide a national infrastructure of community, labor, and religious activists committed to broad-based mobilization campaigns. Consider getting your congregation interested in the fight by checking out worship and action advocacy materials from a variety of faith-based organizations.

Altruistic Traveler: Honor the earth; be resourceful when you travel. Collect hotel bottles of shampoo, conditioner, mouthwash, and bars of soap, and then donate them to a local shelter or prison when you get home. And to keep the home fires burning safely and sustainably, switch to clean-burning soy candles, which provide light from sustainable crops, not polluting sources like oil and uranium.

Peace Be With You: Can't unwind? Overwhelmed? Time crunched? Give yourself the gift of a ten-minute vacation once a day. Pick a specific time and when it arrives, drop everything and sit quietly, eyes closed, emptying your mind of all traffic and distractions for a full ten minutes (set an unobtrusive timer). Inner peace-making takes nurturing, but before long, you'll find yourself looking forward to that pause that refreshes. Your blood pressure, brain, and co-workers will thank you too.

Quitting Time?: Send love home as a messenger before you. On the drive home after work, send a mental message that you are coming home and bringing your love, that you anticipate being home with your loved ones, says Rabbi Zalman Schachter-Shalomi, author of *First Steps to a New Jewish Spirit.* This kind of message is self-fulfilling. By sending it, you consciously commit yourself to the role of giver.

Stop and Statio: Statio is the monastic practice of completely stopping one thing before beginning another, and using that pause to encourage true mindfulness. Let that "time between time" make you a better steward of the earth at the office, even when that office is at home. Use your in-between time to try this laundry experiment: Turn the water temperature the dial to cold/cold. Today's detergents will get your clothes just as clean with cold water as they do with hot water and you'll consume up to 85 percent less energy. In a year, that's equivalent to saving fifty-five gallons of gasoline. Visit Charity Guide(http://charityguide.org/charity/fifteen/laundry.htm) for more information.

Good Works in the WORKPLACE

Women and Children First: Read women's magazines on your lunch hour? Keep reading but switch to a magazine written for women and children. *World Pulse Magazine* is dedicated to unleashing the global power and leadership potential of women and youth (www.worldpulse magazine.com). *World Pulse Magazine* reports on issues such as education, healthcare, refugees, youth peacemakers, and conflict transformation worldwide. Not a word is said about lip gloss or weight loss.

Commute-Lit: Why commute with the crosswords when you can carry a book that could change your life? Two good ones are *In the Footsteps of Gandhi: Conversations with Spiritual Social Activists* by Catherine Ingram and *If the Buddha Came to Dinner: How to Nourish Your Body to Awaken Your Spirit* by Halé Sofia Schatz.

Good Works in the

COMMUNITY

Green Samaritans: You can put your old used cell phone into community action. Collective Good (www.collectivegood.com) will donate your old cell phone to any charity on their list, which includes St. Jude Children's Research Hospital and the Center For Domestic Violence Prevention.

I Was Hungry and You Fed Me: Jesus fasted for forty days. Millions of the world's destitute go hungry daily because they are poor. You and your congregation can help. Join Bread for the World's Offering of Letters campaign (www.bread.org). At Sunday coffee hour, church members can write letters to Congress in support of hunger-fighting legislation, dedicating the letter to God and saying prayers for the hungry worldwide. Bread for the World also has videos available to educate about food justice issues worldwide.

Chapter and Verse Vest: Now you can wear the Word. Prayerware is a line of clothing emblazoned with inspirational quotes as a reminder of the power of prayer. At the website (www.prayerwares.com) you can chat with others whose lives have been empowered by prayer. The company was started by the children of a cancer survivor.

Sundays and Citizenship: Are you observing the Sabbath? Add citizenship to that observance. Participation in the political process is a moral obligation. All major public issues have moral dimensions, just as all religious values have significant public consequences. If you aren't as politically active as you might be, work on it by learning more. Devote Sunday to church *and* citizenship. Read the *Faithful Citizenship* document prepared by the U.S. Catholic Bishops Conference (www.usccb.org/faithfulcitizenship/) and see where your new consciousness leads you.

Be Big, Get Small: Like kneeling, lowering yourself to help a child or an animal is an expression of humility. Do you (like most of us) waste at least an hour a day on trivial pursuits? Keep a journal to find out. Use that wasted hour once a week to mentor a child or walk a dog in an animal shelter. Call your town's social services agency or animal welfare society to get started.

Evangelical Pace-making: Bond with a friend or neighbor and walk daily. It's good for opening the heart spiritually and protecting the heart physically. Make your stroll-mate a male while you're at it. Surveys show men are 20 percent less religious than the opposite sex. If you can get him on his feet, maybe you can get him down on his knees.

Community Investment: "Be filled with all the fullness of God" (Ephesians 3:19). Share some of your fullness with those in need by investing in a community development bank or credit union designed to finance worthwhile projects in low income neighborhoods. You get no-risk market rates and many lending institutions have an environmental focus as well. Visit the Community Investing Center website (www.communityinvest.org) for lists. And if you'd like to do some socially responsible investing (no cigarettes, no munitions, no carcinogenic pharmaceuticals), get started by finding a financial planner in your state at the Social Investment Forum (www.socialinvest.org).

Books for Kids: Doing unto others? Begin with Winnie the Pooh or Robinson Crusoe. The Libri Foundation (www.librifoundation.org) is a nationwide nonprofit which donates new children's books to rural public libraries in the United States through its Books for Children program. Since October 1990 it has donated to

more than 2000 libraries in forty-eight states. You can donate books or buy them through Libri's Wish List at Amazon (www.amazon.com).

Reach Out and Touch Someone: Once a month, instead of phoning friends, write or call your local city and state elected officials and voice your community and environmental concerns. A local voters' league or any search engine will provide names and numbers. Or step out and pitch in on your own home ground. Give up a night of television and go to a town hall meeting. Find out who's fighting the good fight and support them. Or, volunteer to help on a conservation project, anti-litter campaign, or local beautification committee.

Best Bibles: Sharing scripture with the young, the elderly or the literary-challenged? Get a good bible fit. The *King James Version* is written to a twelfth grade reading level, but 40 percent of all adult Christians find it hard to read. The two best bibles for lower reading levels are the *International Children's Bible* and the *New International Reader's Bible*. Mid-level reads are the *Living Bible* and *The Message*.

Overbooked?: Those theological and religious books gathering dust in your den could be a godsend to libraries in prisons and retirement homes and Operation Pass Along operated by SPEAK, Inc. (The Society for Promoting and Encouraging the Arts and Knowledge of the Church) will gladly receive and forward them for you. As a quid pro quo, you can borrow spiritual reads (many out of print or hard-to-find) fee-free from the Operation Pass Along shelves for your own nourishment. Visit SPEAK atwww.speakinc. org.

Your Inner Olympic Coach: The Special Olympics help empower youth and adults with intellectual disabilities to become physically fit through sports training and competition in twenty-six Olympic-style summer and winter sports throughout the world. Sports include everything from archery to floor hockey. Becoming a certified Special Olympics coach involves an easy training program and ongoing continuing education. You don't have to be an athlete. To learn more go to www.special olympics.org.

Class Activism: Are your kids safe from the commercial cleaning products most schools use?

Most are compounded with irritating and allergenic fragrances and chemicals linked to neurological problems, hormone disruptions, and asthma (the leading cause of school absenteeism). There are green alternatives, but your school may not be aware of them. Go to Grassroots Environmental Education's kids and toxins website (www.grassrootsinfo.org/safe schools.html) and read the Childsafe Guidelines to help schools choose healthy and safe cleaning products. Discuss green alternatives with school leadership or consider making a presentation to the PTA. For help and tips, go to the Healthy Schools Network, Inc. (www.healthyschools.org) or The Deirdre Imus Environmental Center for Pediatric Oncology (www.dienviro.com).

To Have or To Have Not: "Examine yourselves," Paul urged the Corinthians (1 Corinthians 11:28), "and only then eat of the bread and drink of the cup." In our have and have not society, some of us have too much while some of us have too little. You can help to correct this imbalance by joining the "Just Food Movement." Three ways to help: support Community Supported Agriculture (www.nal.usda.gov/afsic/csa/csastate.htm), shop at your local farmer's market for local and in-season produce (see the USDA's directory at www.ams.usda.gov/farmersmarkets/map.htm), or give some time and money to the work of Second Harvest (www.secondharvest.org). Once you're educated on the issues, discuss them with your faith community. And last, but not least, express your solidarity with the poor and hungry by fasting once a week or once a month.

SLO Down: "Spiritual practice involves acting out of concern for others' well-being," the Dalai Lama tells us. One way to get with the practice spiritually is to become an activist with Alternatives for Simple Living's SLO (Speakers, Leaders, Organizers) Down Network to spread the word about faith-based voluntary simplicity. Alternatives for Simple Living, whose mission statement is "Equipping people of faith to challenge consumerism, live justly and celebrate responsibly," publishes the popular Christian guide *Whose Birthday Is It Anyway?* and the hymnal *Sing Justice! Do Justice!* For more details, visit www.SimpleLiving.org.

Random Acts of Altruism: Be a twenty-four hour Christian. On your next urban stroll pop a quarter into a nearby meter that's about to expire, drop a few nickels into the mulch under the swings at the playground as buried treasure for the kids to uncover, or place a cut flower under the windshield wiper of a few cars in a nearby parking lot. For more good deed ideas read *Deliberate Acts of Kindness: Service as a Spiritual Practice* by Meredith Gould.

Good Genes: Are you living up to your goodness potential? Do you know what it could be? Practice some brain aerobics while you find out by reading neuroscientist Rhawn Joseph's essay collection *Neurotheology: Brain Science, Spirituality, Religious Experience.* According to Joseph, more than 90 percent of the approximately 31,000 genes in the human genome have yet to be expressed, but it's worth reaching to express them because they contain untold treasures. Practicing the Beatitudes daily could encourage that unfolding.

Beyond the Pink Ribbon: How can you express solidarity with breast cancer victims besides fund-raising walks, pink ribbons, and cash? Consider making a gift of your wedding gown to the Making Memories Breast Cancer Foundation (www.makingmemories.org). Good condition gowns are sold at the foundation's Nationwide Tour of Gowns, while soiled or damaged dresses are turned into quilts which are auctioned off to benefit survivors.

Third Way, Fourth World: The way of Jesus is called the Third Way. Here are two ways to follow the Way. Start by mentoring a child. Take the free online training course at the National Mentoring Partnership website (www.mentoring .org). Then, enter your zip code to find the place, the child, and the opportunity that's right for you. Another place to help poor kids and their parents living in persistent poverty is the Fourth World Movement, a nongovernmental organization with 100,000 volunteer corps in eighty-nine countries plus the United States Their projects include Street Libraries in disadvantaged neighborhoods and an International Workcamp. As a baby step toward fourth world activism, buy a box or two of child-created greeting cards. Even better, sell a carton of them at your next church fair or coffee hour. Visit www.4thworldmovement.org to see the selection and learn more.

A.B.S., Not Us: Forget *People* and *Us*, try *The Record*, the publication of the American Bible Society and the second oldest publication in the United States (www.americanbible.org). You can read copies online, then browse the American Bible Society website for answers to tough scripture questions; get the gospel reading for the day and leave your personal prayer requests, which the American Bible Society will share with its worldwide members. Give answers to others by making a contribution to Samaritans Purse, an American Bible Society ministry which sends bibles to men, women, and children in marginalized areas throughout the world.

As a mother would risk her life to protect her child, So should one cultivate a limitless heart with regard to all beings, With good will for the entire cosmos.

Tipitaka (Theravada Pali Scripture)

Save and Tithe: Can't afford to pay your bills *and* give to charity? Shop at the Unclaimed Baggage Center in Scottsboro, Alabama (www.unclaimedbaggage.com), and pay 80 percent less than list price when you buy that camera, laptop, or tux. The Unclaimed Baggage Center is the store for luggage left behind at depots and airports nationwide. Then, turn that 20 percent savings over to an agency where it can do some good, helping victims of disasters like earthquakes, droughts, and famine. Another way to save and tithe is to barter what you don't need for what you do. Check out the possibilities at Family Trader (www.familytrader.com).

Give to the Needy: "You always have the poor with you," Jesus tells us in John 12:8. Jesus calls us to see the poor in our midst rather than looking away. The poor in spirit, the disenfranchised, the marginalized, they all show us Christ's presence in our midst. Choose a way to consciously respond to the poor in your community once a week by bringing food to the food pantry, working at the soup kitchen or hospitality house, or mentoring a needy child or lonely senior. Even better, enlist your parish to adopt an ongoing project that benefits one of these causes.

The Paws That Refreshes:

"Goodness is uneventful," Christian counselor David Grayson once observed. "It does not flash, it glows." Sometimes it even barks, when that goodness comes from being a volunteer puppy raiser for the Guiding Eyes for the Blind (www.guidingeyes.org), a nonprofit nation-wide organization that trains animal lovers to bring up a puppy that at maturity will become a blind person's seeing eyes. Guiding Eyes for the Blind provides mandatory classes, local area coordinators, reimbursement for vet expenses, and a healthy specially-bred pup. You provide the T.L.C.

Real Cool: What's an evolved Joe College alternative to hazing, flashing, and bashing? Visit the Idealist on Campus program of Action Without Borders (www.idealist.org/ioc) if you have a collegian in the house. The national non-profit is designed to engage students in improving communities and considering ways to stay involved throughout their lifetimes. Idealist on Campus values the power that college students and their campuses have to strengthen communities and the world at large.

Faith-based Voting: Vote with your religious values. Learn more about the issues in national elections from a religious perspective and the voting process in general at: NETWORK, A National Catholic Social Justice Lobby (www.net worklobby.org), the National Priorities Project (www.nationalpriorities.org), and Peace Action (www.peace-action.org).

Good Works in

SOCIETY

Is Life Speed-bump Free Where You Are?:
Say thanks by helping someone whose life is
hanging in the balance. Go to the Crisis Relief
corner at www.networkforgood.org, where you
can learn where and how to give blood, become
a member of the Citizens Corps Community
Emergency Response Team in your town, work as
a U.S. Forest Service volunteer in fire devastated
areas, and more. If you're not sure where to lend

a helping hand, sign up for the *Network for Good* newsletter to hear about current crises and needy causes.

The Helping Hand Habit: "No act of kindness, no matter how small, is ever wasted," observed Aesop, the fifth century fabulist. Are you volunteering on a regular basis through your church or community center? Besides what it does for others, the habit of altruism boosts immunity, lessens depression and fatigue, and improves self-esteem. If you don't know where to start, visit Volunteer Match (www.volunteermatch.org) where you can research various opportunities and find your match.

New Cotton Bowl: Ready for a new cotton tee or a school sweatshirt? Make it an organic tee to save the environment and the workers in the fields. According to 1995 data, U.S. farmers applied nearly one-third of a pound of chemical fertilizers and pesticides for every pound of cotton harvested. Some of these chemicals are among the most toxic classified by the U.S. Environmental Protection Agency. Learn more about fair-trade organic cotton clothing by clicking up Beneficial T's by Patagonia at www.beneficialts.com. And to learn more about the issues, visit The Worker Rights Consortium (www.workersrights.org).

Write a Letter, Save an Animal: "Until we stop harming all living beings, we are still savages," said Thomas Edison. If you'd like to spare a few of the billions of animals who are slaughtered yearly, sign up for Kinship Circle's Letter Library. A letter service for animal lovers who are too busy to write the letters that are in their hearts, the Letter Library creates hundreds of letters yearly which are e-mailed or mailed to legislators and newspapers on behalf of animal victims of rodeos, zoos, vivisection labs, hunting, factory farms, and more. To see sample letters, fact sheets, and learn more, visit Kinship Circle (www.kinshipcircle.org).

The New Power of One: "As we do what we are here on earth to do, it is critical to remember that we are part of something bigger in ways that we never know," says Frances Moore Lappé, the author of *Hope's Edge*. Learn more about how to be a power of one in the twenty-first century from the Small Planet Fund (http://smallplanetfund.org), which supports and reports on citizen-led solutions to poverty, hunger, and environmental devastation around the world.

Just Jeans and More: Need a shirt, tote, or hoodie for the kids? Get them with a clear conscience at No Sweat (www.nosweatshop .com), which sells nothing but union-made non-sweatshop apparel. The site offers brands such as Union Jean and Sweat X. Another site for socially responsible shopping is Justice Clothing Co. (www.justiceclothing.com).

Sight Seconds: Donate an old pair of eye glasses or prescription sunglasses to the Lions Club International Foundation (www.lionsclubs .org), whose vision programs donate five million pairs of glasses a year to needy children, adults, and seniors in this country and abroad. The Lions Club also supports eye care clinics and vision screenings and supplies Braille Readers and Seeing Eye dogs. Check the website for a drop-off location near you.

Pray for Peace, but Befriend a Person in Uniform: Whether you're a total pacifist or believe in the Just War Theory, the fact remains that some of our countrymen are in the armed forces and in harm's way. If you've never known one, get in touch by e-mail or snail mail and discover some common ground, whatever your politics. Go to America Supports You (www.americasupportsyou.mil) or Operation Dear Abby (http://anyser vicemember.navy.mil) for details.

Books behind Bars: Incarceration and illiteracy go together. Books can break the bond. Prisoners are especially eager for new or used reference books, how-to texts, health and legal books, books in Spanish, and books on faith and personal growth. Send them to:
Books Behind Bars
4722 Baltimore Avenue
Philadelphia, PA 19143
(writeaprisoner.com/books-behind-bars.htm)

Or send books on women's recovery issues, women's health, parenting, fiction by women of color, and school texts including GED prep materials to:

Women's Prison Book Project
c/o Arise Bookstore
2441 Lyndale Ave., S.
Minneapolis, MN 55405
(www.prisonactivist.org/wpbp/)

Next time you buy a book for yourself (or pick up several at a tag sale or church fair), buy one for our brothers and sisters behind bars, too.

Help the Helpers: More than 5,000 Franciscan missionaries around the world serve the sick, the poor, the aged, and the lepers in Asia, Africa, and Latin America through the nonprofit organization Franciscan Missions, Inc. Your $10 contribution helps God's helpers, and in return, the missionaries will say mass for you or anyone you designate. Triduums, novenas, and Gregorian masses can also be requested. For more information, visit the Franciscan Missions website (www.franciscanmissions.org/MassForm.htm).

The More We Love: "Love measures our stature; the more we love, the bigger we are. There is no smaller package in all the world than that of a man wrapped up in himself," said civil rights Freedom Rider and nuclear disarmament activist William Sloane Coffin. You could grow in stature by supporting the work of Fellowship of Reconciliation (www.forusa.org), an interfaith and international movement with branches and groups in more than forty countries and on every continent. Representing all faith traditions and none, Fellowship of Reconciliation seeks nonviolent responses to conflict and reconciliation through compassionate action. Membership also allows you to join one of the many fellowships they sponsor as well as a local Fellowship of Reconciliation group in your area.

Do not neglect to do good and share what you have.

Hebrews 13:16

Pause for Paws: Feed fourteen homeless hungry animals today by purchasing what you need (clothes, jewelry, gifts, etc.) from the Greater Good Network Store (www.gearthatgives.com). Among other charities they work with, Greater Good donates fourteen bowls of food to animals living in shelters and sanctuaries for every purchase you make through Animal Rescue Online (www.animalrescue.com). In 2003, visitors funded almost fourteen million bowls of pet food to Animal Rescue Online.

Far from the Sabbath: Americans' productivity grows by 3 percent a year, says the American Heart Association. And although taking an annual vacation reduces the risk of heart attack by 50 percent, fewer and fewer of us get the getaway we need. Say no to busyness; join the Simplicity Forum(www.simpleliving.net/simpli cityforum/default.asp), a leadership alliance that seeks to promote simplicity in our work and to actively change the culture and policies that drive over-work and over-consumption. The forum sponsors conferences on sustainability, social justice, spirit, and the annual Take Back Your Time Day. A good read to get you started on the simplicity path is *In Praise of Slowness: How A Worldwide Movement Is Challenging the Cult of Speed* by Carl Honore.

Just Checking: Put your money where your spirit is. Use imprinted checks from Message Checks (www.messageproducts.com) that speak up for social justice and the environment every time you pay a bill. Organizations represented by Message Checks include everything from Amnesty International to Mothers Against Drunk Driving. Checks printed on recycled paper are thriftier than bank-issued types. Business cards and labels are also available.

Mouse to Mouth: Every 3.5 seconds someone somewhere dies of hunger and 24,000 people die every day from hunger or hunger-related causes. Six million children under the age of five die every year from hunger. But each time you visit The Hunger Site (www.thehungersite.com) someone is fed, thanks to the site's corporate sponsors. Even better, you can come back for seconds and each visit puts rice in someone's bowl. For greater hunger-relief, make multiple copies of the homepage and leave it in restaurants, coffee shops, wherever you grab that bite that others are denied.

Imani and Me: Could your Sunday School curriculum use a makeover? Consider Church World Service's *Build a Better World* with inspiring stories of children from Sudan, Bolivia, Afghanistan, and Mexico, integrated with Bible studies, activities, handouts, and posters. There are also T-shirts and stickers featuring the curriculum mascot, Imani the giraffe. See the website(www.churchworldservice.org/kids/Ed0005/introduction.htm) to order or for more information.

Rapid Response: "Where there is hatred, let me sow love," vowed St. Francis. "Where there is despair, let me bring hope." You can get started doing both by joining a faith-based legislative action network to keep updated on bills before Congress. Two good ones: e-mail Pax Christi's Rapid Response network (paxwpb@gate.net) or visit NETWORK, A National Catholic Social Justice Lobby (www.networklobby.org).

Save a Life before Lunch: Hunger is a bread and butter issue. Keep your pen next to your bread knife. Become a lay lobbyist for Bread for the World (www.bread.org), the nationwide Christian movement seeking to end world hunger by the end of the century by lobbying the nation's decision makers. Subscribe to the Bread for the World newsletter and keep it at your dining table to remind you to take the suggested action of the month. Bread for the World members write, call, and visit  members of congress, support hunger activism, and sponsor an annual Offering of Letters campaign.

Peaces of Eight: There are self-centered ways to spend $8 and heart-centered ways. You could buy two large lattes today or you could drink water and spend the money on "The Spirit of Peace," a moving seventy-minute documentary about the life of the twentieth century activist known as Peace Pilgrim. Peace Pilgrim walked the world with nothing but a backpack, spreading the message of love and peace. For this and other related tapes, books, and videos, visit the Peace Pilgrim website (http://peacepilgrim.org).

Create Your Own Personal WWJD Day: On that day, imagine what Jesus would do if he lived in your community—and do it. First pick an issue or area—local schools, your church, a soup kitchen or shelter, or the local conservation society; or read the local papers through Jesus' eyes and choose a problem to respond to as you imagine Jesus might. Then turn up and be his stand-in.

Fast with Strangers in Christ: Twice a month on the first and fifteenth, the Word Made Flesh community ("Serving Jesus among the Poor of the Poor") fasts as a way of petitioning the Lord on behalf of the poor and all his laborers. You are invited to join them, humbling your heart in self examination, to give away what you would have eaten for the day, and to give of yourself to those in need. Word Made Flesh ministries serves South America, South Asia, and Eastern Europe including abused women in Nepal, homeless street kids in Peru, and urban youth in Romania. Go to the Word Made Flesh website(www.word

madeflesh.com) to learn about the "Incarnational methodology" behind the Word Made Flesh ministry and subscribe to their inspiring (free) quarterly advocacy journal *The Cry.*

Knit One, Compassion Too: Is knitting a spiritual practice? Find out by reading *Zen and the Art of Knitting: Exploring the Links Between Knitting, Spirituality, and Creativity* by Bernadette Murphy to pick up lore, tips, and designs. Then get altruistically inspired and join Afghans for Afghans (www.afghansforafghans .org), a humanitarian project that accepts hand-knitted or crocheted sweaters, blankets, hats, and slippers and delivers them to needy men, women, and children in war-torn Afghanistan.

Barter Redux: Do you believe in community sustainability? Do you like the share-and-share-alike idea? Plug into the fast-growing alternative currency movement that creates a local currency which maintains community trade regardless of the fluctuations of money and employment in local economies. Members barter goods and services indirectly, using currency approximate in value to one unit of the national currency with a computer system to do the banking. Alternatively, you can earn credits through your labor and trade them for the goods and services of others. All you need is a church, neighborhood association, or other community enterprise. For more info, go to Time Dollar USA (www.timedollar.org).

The Social Justice Cusp: Is your church on the cusp of social justice? It could be, if it subscribes to *Sojomail* a weekly e-mail-zine of spirituality, politics, and culture from Sojourners (www.sojo.net). The website is also the home of *Sojourners* magazine. Each issue addresses social justice issues (poverty, hunger, sweatshops, etc.) from the Christian perspective including background, reflections on the issues, and suggested actions.

Read (and Pray) All about It: Have you seen today's headlines according to Public Citizen, the Sierra Club, Camp for Tobacco-Free Kids, or Punkvoter.org? How about Women's E-news? Among other topics, you can learn about Pakistan's "cradle babies," the 1,500 infants, largely girls, who are discarded yearly by parents too impoverished to care for them; and about Pakistan's Edhi Foundation, which since 1975 has rescued 15,000 infants. Pray for Pakistan's babies and keep up with all the rest of the under-reported news of the day by subscribing to the daily e-list at the Common Dreams website (www.commondreams.org), which covers news for the progressive community worldwide.

Non-Specieist Compassion: Did you know that for every egg you eat, a hen spends thirty hours confined and immobilized in a battery cage? To learn more about understanding and reversing human violence to nonhuman animals, read *You Can Save the Animals: 251 Simple Ways to Stop Thoughtless Cruelty* by PETA president Ingrid Newkirk.

Ladies First: Quick—can you name America's top-rated female chess player? Do you know of at least one prominent woman mathematician besides Julia Robinson? Can you locate Avenger Field, history's only all-female air-cadet base? If you can't answer these questions, you need to enrich your life with stuff from the National Women's History Project (www.nwhp.org), which celebrates women's history and achievements with everything from multicultural coloring books to a "Courageous Voices" afghan.

The National Women's History Project, which sponsors National Women's History Month, was founded in 1980 to recognize and celebrate the historic accomplishments of women in all fields.

What Would Paul Do?: "Devote yourselves to prayer, keeping alert in it with thanksgiving," Paul advised the Colossians (Colossians 4:2). One thing to be watchful of (and pray about) are sweatshops that deprive their workers (often children and teenagers working long hours in harsh conditions for poverty wages) of rights and dignity. And one thing to be thankful for is sweatshop alternatives where you can buy clothes that were created fairly, in humane conditions, at decent wages. Go to The Clean Clothes Connection (www.clean clothesconnection.org) and click on "Shop for a Better World." Read "Q & A's about Sweatshops" to get the complete lowdown on this unjust system.

Civic Duty Made Official: When was the last time you gave the president or your congresspersons a piece of your mind? There are organizations that can mediate that dialogue and even give you a sample letter (to alter as needed) on important issues of the day which you can e-mail, fax or mail fee-free. Sign up for e-mail updates on critical legislation from NETWORK, A National Catholic Social Justice Lobby (www.networklobby.org). Or visit Public Citizen (www.publiccitizen.org) or MoveOn.org Civic Action (www.moveon.org).

Go to Prison This Year: "Remember those who are in prison, as though you were in prison with them; those who are being tortured, as though you yourselves were being tortured," the book of Hebrews requests (13:3). As a volunteer in the Kairos Prison Ministry program, you'll spend a three-day weekend in retreat, as a member of a team, sharing meals and fellowship with prisoners on a one-to-one basis. Subsequent visits are half-day reunions with the prisoners over a twelve-month period. For details, visit the Kairos Prison Ministry website (www.kairos prisonministry.org) and check the ministry map for the program in your neighborhood.

The Culture Zone: Get outside your comfort zone one night a week. Even better, get outside your cultural time zone. What do you know about Middle Eastern social issues—the environment, human rights, economics? We are all connected, so it matters. Start by boning up on the work of activist Sema Samar and her support of Afghan and Pakistani women and children, including the establishment of girl's schools and hospitals through her organization Shuhada (www.shuhada.org). Consider supporting the work of Shuhada by purchasing a native rug, tablecloth, or bed linens (and more) at the Support Shuhada Organization website, (http://support.shuhada.org/index.php).

Christmas on the Other Side: We all remember the child in the manger at Christmas, but what about the child whose parent is behind bars? A donation to Prison Fellowship's Angel Tree Program (www.angeltree.org) will put gifts (plus the Gospel story of the first Christmas) under the trees of children with incarcerated parents. A donation of as little as $8.52 (the price of a fast-food lunch) will help one child thanks to Angel Tree's extensive network of volunteers and churches.

How's Your Credit?: "I will grant peace in the land," God tells us in Leviticus 26:6 . But the self-sufficiency part is up to us. Mindful that 50 percent of the world's people live on $2 a day or less and 20 percent on less than one dollar, Oikocredit (www.oikocredit.org/site/en.),founded by the World Council of Churches in 1975, has been providing micro credit to poor communities throughout Asia, Africa and Latin America to promote self-sufficiency. You can help. A minimum investment is $1,000, but the paybacks are plentiful.

The Least of These: "I was naked and you gave me clothing. . . . Truly I tell you, just as you did it to one of the least of these who are members of my family, you did it to me," Jesus said in Matthew 25:36, 40. This includes the smallest of all God's children, newborns. One way to show T.L.C. to him and them: donate baby clothes or baby supplies (including patterns and sewing notions) to Newborns in Need (www.newbornsin need.org). Other suggestions for helping Newborns in Need include starting a local chapter, or holding a toy drive. Or send a handmade baby quilt to ABC Quilts for an at-risk infant (born HIV-positive, or affected by the mother's alcohol or drug abuse). Even better, join ABC's network of home quilters (they'll teach you what you need to know) and sew with an infant in mind. Send for their educational package at www.abcquilts.org.

P.O.C. T.L.C.: If you've fed the hungry or clothed the naked, try donating one lunch hour a week to write to a prisoner of conscience and express your support. For a list of Catholic peace activists serving sentences for various antiwar actions, go to the School of the Americas Watch website (www.soaw.org/new/article.php?id=322).

Grand Good Deed: "What you do to the least of these, you do to me," said Jesus. Live out this invitation by mentoring a disadvantaged child or becoming a foster grandparent. Open to men and women over sixty, as a volunteer you'll work with an at-risk or special needs child through a variety of community organizations. The program is part of the Senior Corps (www.seniorcorps.org).

Walk for Your Health: Walk for someone else's health while you're at it. Join in the nearest CROP walk in your community or help organize one through your worship community. Sponsored by Church World Service, there are 2,000 interfaith community crop walks yearly throughout the country. Funds raised are used to stop hunger around the world through self-help development initiatives. To learn more, visit the Church World Service website (www.churchworldservice .org/CROP). And while you're there, order one of their calendars, which offer a look at CROP in action throughout the world—from the slums of Mozambique to the back streets of Florida.

Bread, Not Stones: "Is there anyone among you who, if your child asks for bread, will give a stone?" Jesus asks us (Matthew 7:9). Apparently the U.S. government qualifies. Only six cents is spent on education and four cents on healthcare for every fifty cents that is spent on the military. In fact, the U.S. spends nearly seventeen times as much on defense as the combined total spent by the six countries most often identified by the Pentagon as our potential adversaries. To vote for bread not stones, join the Bread, Not Stones campaign organized by Pax Christi USA, the national Catholic peace movement (www. paxchristiusa.org/pc_bread_stones.asp). Say no to the insatiable appetite for more and better weapons and yes to the development of new strategies for lasting peace.

Beyond Babe: Farm animals suffer because of the inhumane agribusiness practices that threaten both human and inhuman lives. Animals are confined tightly in warehouses where they cannot exercise or engage in natural behaviors. They are  under constant stress, are poorly nourished, and are fed toxic drugs. You can help by becoming a voice for the voiceless. Join Farm Sanctuary (www.farmsanctuary.org) and receive regular action alerts. A contribution of $20 or more entitles you to a Farm Sanctuary Membership for one year. Your contribution supports legal advocacy, legislative projects, cruelty investigations, media outreach, public awareness and humane education projects, and direct rescue and shelter efforts for abused farm animals. And to learn more about the abuses of factory farming, read *Dominion: The Power of Man, the Suffering of Animals, and the Call to Mercy* by Matthew Scully.

The New Abolition Movement: As of 2001, there were more than 3700 men and women on death row throughout the U.S. If you agree with the National Conference of Bishops that "the death penalty offers the tragic illusion that we can defend life by taking it," visit the Campaign to End the Death Penalty (www.nodeathpenalty.org). While you're there, read "5 Reasons to Oppose the Death Penalty," one of which is racism (75 percent of all federal death row prisoners are non-white). Also, click up *The New Abolitionist*, the campaign's monthly newsletter.

Black Marks, Greyhounds: Man's best friend, if he's a greyhound and a racer, gets less than the best treatment. According to the Fund for Animals, thousands of dogs are killed (or often maimed or electrocuted) yearly in a system that puts profits first. Many dogs are badly injured while competing, or are killed outright when no longer profitable. Greyhounds are even cruelly treated while racing, caged for up to twenty-two hours, fed cheap chow, and forced to perform on the hottest summer and coldest winter days. Lend a hand though The Greyhound Project (www.adopt-a-greyhound.org) or become a real activist and adopt a retired racer through one of the site's agencies. To learn about human cruelty to other animals, visit the Fund for Animals (www.fundforanimals.org) and become a Humane Activist.

So then, whenever we have an opportunity, let us work for the good of all.

Galatians 6:10

ISM (Instant Spiritual Messaging): Timid about speaking up? Wear a tee that expresses something you believe in your soul, even if (especially if) it's controversial (are you pro-life, against leather, anti-war?), it may spark conversation and give you a chance to win a few converts to your favorite cause or movement. Go to Syracuse Cultural Workers (www.syrcultural workers.com) or the Donnelly/Colt Progressive

Resources Catalog (www.donnellycolt.com) to shop for buttons, tees, bumper stickers, and posters.

Save the Ducks: "In happiness and suffering," goes the Jainism golden rule, "we should regard all creatures as our own self." All creatures means everyone including web-footed ducks and geese, hundreds of thousands of which are confined in dark sheds, and cruelly force-fed each year to produce the "gourmet" delicacy, foie gras. This barbaric process forces the liver to expand ten times its natural size and often results in the premature death of these gentle creatures. Speak out for the suffering of our feathered friends. Join the campaign to stop force-feeding cruelty by visiting www.nofoiegras.org (a Farm Sanctuary campaign) and urge your favorite restaurant to stop serving this product of animal suffering.

Give, Give, Give: Children with music education perform better and develop better math and problem solving skills than nonmusical children. If you've got an unused instrument gathering dust, donate it to the music education department at your local school. Or think sports. Used golf clubs can be donated to the Clubs for Kids program sponsored by the Professional Golfers' Association of America (www.pga.org). They will be used to teach golf to kids who would be unable to afford equipment and lessons.

All the News That's Really Fit to Print: You can get the news with God and real ethics factored in for only twenty-five cents a year, in *The Catholic Worker.* Full of insightful social journalism at its most responsible, the eight-times-a-year newspaper has been printing for more than half a century. And you don't have to be a Catholic to reap the rewards. Recent articles included coverage of the war in Iraq, a tribute to the pipe organ, and a look at homelessness in New York City. Write The Catholic Worker, 36 East First St., New York, NY 10003 to subscribe (and consider a generous contribution to keep journalism's best-kept secret going).

Reuse Your Shoes: Transitioning to a new pair of sneaks? Do the right thing and turn them into a soccer field or a running track. That's what happens when you send your used athletic shoes to the Nike Reuse-A-Shoe project (www.nikereuseashoe.com). And if you're buying new shoes, invest in PVC (vinyl) free ones. Vinyl is a dangerous volatile toxin that threatens the health of the workers who make them, and some shoe manufacturers (Puma, Reebok, and Nike among them) are eliminating it. To learn more on clothing company practices in general, visit the Fair Labor Association (www.fairlabor.org/all/transparency).

Trust in the LORD, and do good. . . .

Psalm 37:3

Good Works in the ENVIRONMENT

The Gospel and Global Warming: What has your congregation done to save the earth from global warming lately? If the answer is "not much," introduce it to "One God, One Family, One Earth: Responding to the Gifts of God's Creation," a six session adult education curriculum to help us rediscover our relationship with God's creation. It's available to read by mail order through Eco-Justice Programs National Council of Churches (www.nccecojustice.org).

Get Your Hands Dirty: Celebrate peace and look forward to spring with your family by creating a garden in the fall using twelve different kind of bulbs to represent each of the world's religions. For example, daffodils stand for Christianity, and red tulips stand for Judaism. If you have space, try planting a tree or shrub in the center of the garden bed to represent the one God who unites us. Plan a planting ritual—reading aloud one prayer from each tradition as you put the bulbs in the earth. You can find the prayers that were used on the UN's Day of Prayer for World Peace in 1986 at www.souledout.org/newworldreligion/worldpray ers/peaceprayers.html. To make a smaller garden, celebrate six faiths and use flower boxes or planters for a porch or patio. Keep a folder with the prayers at a spot near the garden to use once a week.

Godly Home and Garden: "God has arranged all things in the world in consideration of everything else," said Hildegard of Bingen, a twelfth-century theologian and visionary. Using toxic pesticides and herbicides in our homes and gardens threatens that delicate divine balance. Find out whether there are dangerous ingredients in the products you use at the Natural Resources Defense Council website (www.nrdc.org) or the Pesticide Action Network's Pesticides Database (www.pesticideinfo.org). And for green alternatives visit The Green Guide (www.thegreenguide.com).

Take a Bath (Not a Shower): A five-minute shower sends fifty gallons of water down the drain. A simple showerhead attachment, costing less than a week's supply of bottled water, can reduce flow to three gallons per minute. Or, how about sliding into the sensuous pleasure of a hot and healthy tub bath. Add Epsom salts or aromatherapy oils and listen to spiritual music while you soak and de-stress. For a music catalog visit Credence Communications (www.credencecommunications.com) or Sounds True (www.soundstrue.com).

Tapping the Tap: Did you know that using water conservation tricks at home cuts your bill and reduces the need to dam another river? Turn these water wasters into savers:

- Take a shorter shower and use a low-flow shower head to cut water use by 75 percent;
- Invest in a toilet dam to cut flushed water by 50 percent;
- Replace the small screen in your faucet with a faucet aerator to reduce water flow by 60 percent.

Tall Timber Concerns: Show your tall timber concerns. Two trees supply the oxygen needs of a person each year. Trees, shrubs, and grass all produce life-giving oxygen and help prevent soil erosion. Plant a tree, shrub, or herb plant each year on your birthday to give back to the earth which gives to you. Also try using unbleached unscented and uncolored toilet and facial tissues. The dyes and bleach in these products pollute waterways. Microwave heated paper plates pollute your body with large amounts of carcinogenic dioxin. To learn more about dioxin go to Health Care Without Harm (www.noharm.org/pvcDehp/dioxin).

Dispense with Disposables: When you do use single service paperware choose biodegradable paper, not ozone-destructive laminated plastics and polystyrene. Switch to wax paper in place of environmentally-hostile tinfoil and plastic wrap. And use re-usable sponges for cleanup instead of paper towels. Buy and use cloth, not paper napkins that put toxic dioxin into the environment. And to develop a deeper appreciation of the meaning of stewardship of the earth, read Vandana Shiva's *The Violence of the Green Revolution: Third World Agriculture, Ecology and Politics.*

Yes to Freecycle, No to Landfills: Do you have an old bicycle, snowblower, or treadmill on its last legs? Forget the landfill and post a message at the Freecycle message board (www.free cycle.org) to connect with someone else who may be willing to take your stuff in exchange for something they're giving away. There are currently more than 3,034 Freecycle groups in forty-eight countries that have kept countless tons of stuff out of our nation's overstuffed landfills.

Second Time Around: Some things you can't (or shouldn't) junk or recycle. Mirrors are one. But you can give them a second life by donating them to a nonprofit through the Reuse Development Organization (www.redo.org).

The Power of ONE

Acting and Activism: Turn your kids into activists. Send them to Leonardo DiCaprio's website (www.leonardodicaprio.org), operated by the ecoconscious actor to encourage young people to vote, write letters of protest, and learn about issues like global warming, sustainability, biodiversity, and more. Kids can also keep up with all the green holidays like November 26: Buy Nothing Day and November 15: America Recycles Day.

Green Goods: "Walk Softly and leave a light footprint," urge the Native Americans. You can start small with the everyday details like grooming products. Look for manufacturers who care enough to use certified organic and non-endangered ingredients, and materials not tested in animals. Go to the home of Aveda hair and skincare products (www.aveda.com) to learn how an eco-minded company does business responsibly.

Smart Mail: Sending packages overnight or by two-day air creates five times the greenhouse gases of ordinary parcel post. There are earth-friendlier ways to shop and send. At holiday times, get together with a friend and have both of your orders sent to one address. Cancel catalogs if the company you're dealing with has a website. Rather than a home address, which may not be on the regular UPS or other carrier's route, save gas and expense and have your packages sent to your business address, which is on a regular route.

Bless the Earth Bike!: Are you part of the pollution solution? Cars are the single largest source of air pollution, causing 79 percent of the toxic carbon monoxide in the atmosphere. Not able to switch to a green car (yet)? How about a green bike? Driving less and biking for shorter trips reduces global warming, which impacts animal, human, and plant life. A daily four-mile round trip by bike (rather than car) prevents 185 pounds of pollution from being released annually.

The Greening of the Green: Be the green golfer you were meant to be. Join the Audubon Society's Cooperative Sanctuary Program—

a win/win movement aimed at replacing a percentage of the country's turf on golf clubs with native grass, thereby inviting back wildlife, reducing water and chemical use and maintenance, and putting putters back into a nature-as-nature-was-intended-to-be setting. Non-golfer's can participate in the Sustainable Communities Program, taking a pledge to make a difference where they live. In return for your pledge, the Audubon Society will help you improve the quality of your environment— from birds and butterflies to waterways and wetlands. For more information, visit Audubon International at www.audubonintl.org.

Ethical Pleasures: Do you love fresh flowers? Buy them organically grown to avoid the pesticides. Ten to a hundred times more pesticides are used on flowers than on fruits and vegetables. Pesticides endanger the health of greenhouse workers, especially in the developing countries from which many cut flowers come. For details visit Organic Bouquet (www.organicbouquet.com).

Dangerous Cocoa: Chocolate is another treat that is no treat for the workers who harvest it (including slave and child labor) and the rainforests that are decimated to make way for it. Switch to Fair Trade organic chocolate, which ensures a living wage for farmers and protects the rainforest. Visit the Global Exchange website to learn about the dangers involved in cocoa farming (www.globalexchange.org/campaigns/fairtrade/cocoa/).

Discard unto Others: One day a month review your bounty and tithe a part of it. Pass clothes, furniture, kitchenware, and toys that have served their purpose in your home on to a second life in someone else's. Nursery schools, libraries, thrift shops, soup kitchens, shelters, and relatives are all potential next-in-line users. Turn  over packing peanuts to the local UPS store, unused hangers to the cleaners, and egg cartons and plastic jugs to the local kindergarten or nursery school.

Gas Free Getaways: Cars are the largest source of urban air pollution, generating more than two-thirds of the carbon monoxide in the atmosphere, a third of the nitrogen oxides, and a quarter of the hydrocarbons. Cars are also less safe than public transportation. You are actually forty times safer traveling by train than by car. To avoid environmental pollution and traffic jams, consider some options such as biking, ferries, metro buses, and interurban train lines and Amtrak (which offers city to city service with subway links). Check out Rail-to-Trails Conservancy (www.railstrails.org), The Public Purpose (www.publicpurpose.com), and the American Public Transportation Association (www.publictransportation.org/systems) for more information and travel ideas.

Eco-Auto: Be a car owner with an eco-conscience: Have regular tune-ups, change your air and oil filters regularly, and recycle your used motor oil at your local service station. Also, pipe down: keep your muffler and tailpipe in good condition to reduce noise pollution and make sure you're properly equipped with properly functioning antipollution devices. Last, but not least, invest in a car that gives the greatest efficiency for the lowest horsepower, and start saving for an electric hybrid.

Green Power, Not Greenhouse Gas: American households are responsible for more greenhouse emissions than driving cars—9900 pounds of carbon dioxide a year. Halt that planetary-trashing trend by going green. More than 500 utility companies in thirty-three states now offer green power, derived from renewable sources rather than fossil fuels. You pay your utility company to either produce or purchase a certain amount of renewable energy from the sun, wind, plants, water, and other natural sources. To learn more, read The Green Power Product Report (www.greenguide.com).

Waste Not, Mail Not: American catalog companies send out seventeen billion catalogs (fifty-nine for each person in the U.S.) each year. If the industry included just 10 percent post-consumer recycled pulp, 85,000 tons of wood would be saved. You can help by saying no to the stream of catalogs to your mailbox. Register with the Direct Mail Association's Mail Preference Service to reduce catalogs and unsolicited mail (www.dmaconsumers.org/cgi/offmailinglist).

Winging It: Flying may be cheaper than ever, but it's costlier on the environment, causing air and noise pollution and increasing greenhouse gas emissions (which are expected to double by 2020!). Since guidelines on international air travel are excluded from the Kyoto Protocol (an international treaty on global warming), changes from the airline industry may be a long time in coming. In the meantime, opt for train rather than plane, when you can. For example, traveling from London to Amsterdam by train rather than plane reduces CO_2 emissions by 300 percent. To learn more about international train travel, visit EcoBusinessLinks Environmental Directory (www.ecobusinesslinks.com/train_travel_directory.htm).

Beach-bound?: Be a green sun seeker. Our oceans are going down the drain, says the U.S. Commission on Ocean Policy. The commission reports that eighty-two species of fish and twenty-eight marine mammal species have become depleted, endangered, or threatened. Also, 40,000 acres of coastal wetlands disappear annually because of human development. Be a good beach steward—bring garbage bags and dispose of your litter properly and don't spill anything into the ocean containing chemicals. When you get home, learn how you can do even more at Oceans Alive (www.oceansalive.org).

For the LORD your God is God of gods and Lord of lords, the great God, mighty and awesome . . . who executes justice for the orphan and the widow, and who loves the strangers, providing them food and clothing.

Deuteronomy: 10:17-18

E-Waste Not: If your PC isn't green, it doesn't compute, ethically or ecologically. Only 10 percent of the more than 250 million PCs that will become obsolete this year will be recycled or reconditioned. The other 90 percent make our landfills toxic. PCs are built from hazardous materials and create hazardous waste upon disposal. A typical cathode ray tube monitor contains five to seven pounds of lead, a neurotoxin. Don't add to the e-waste. Get in touch with the Computer TakeBack Campaign (www.computertakeback.com) to learn about buying recycling issues, and to see the Environmental Protection Agency's e-cycling website (www.epa.gov/epaoswer/hazwaste/recycle/ecycling/index.htm) for information on eco-sound recycling.

Alternative Agribusiness: Did you know that the food for the average American meal travels an average of 1300 miles, doing nothing to keep prices reasonable or promote the local economy? If you're fed up, look into Community Supported Agriculture, a unique way to reconnect with your food and the land through direct relationships with farmers and local farms. Through Community Supported Agriculture, communities purchase shares in a farm. Shareholders are entitled to set amounts of organic produce during the growing season. Shareholders also share in the financial risk of farming, but the guaranteed income means growers can focus on growing high-quality food rather than cash crops. Click up the Community Supported Agriculture website (www.nal.usda.gov/afsic/csa) for more details on a farm near you.

Green Deed: Greet spring with a green good deed: plant a tree. Did you know that a single tree removes 8,000 pounds of carbon dioxide from the atmosphere during its lifetime and combats global warming? No place for a tree of your own? Visit Trees for the Future (www.treesftf.org) where a membership fee of $40 will pay for the planting of 400 trees in tree-deficient communities around the world. An even bigger green deed? Have a grove of trees planted (for only $100!) in one of seven countries including Honduras, Haiti, and India, in the name of a friend or relative.

Take a Stand for Trees: Forests are home to two-thirds of the world's land based species of

plants and animals, but 70 percent are seriously threatened by commercial logging interests. You can help change this trend by supporting Greenpeace (www.greenpeace.org). The organization documents logging practices and pressures major importers and retail stores to reward responsible wood  producers and reject illegal logging. Two easy take-back-the-forests acts: refrain from buying wood products that are not certified by the Forest

Stewardship Council, and insist that your elected officials call for proper global forest management.

Care of Creation: Are environmental problems spiritual problems? If you don't think so, or if you aren't sure, send for a free copy of *Creation Care Magazine* from the Evangelical Environmental Network (www.creationcare.org), a ministry seeking scripture-based solutions to environmental problems. While you're there, read and sign on to the Evangelical Declaration on the Care of Creation (you don't have to be an evangelical).

Healthy, Wealthy, and Wise: You could be all three if you kick your dependence on plastic. Plastic is produced from nonrenewable petroleum and also releases toxic substances when heated that migrate into food. Drink tap water (from a thermos) instead of buying plastic bottles, and replace items like Tupperware and plastic utensils, which are costly and wasteful, with glass containers and flatware, which are eco-friendly and healthier than plastic.

Good Works in the
GLOBAL
COMMUNITY

Spiritual Food: "The cultural identity of people is closely connected with food" says Maria Mies writing in the Peaceworker. "And if that is handed over to the multinational corporations which produce food industrially this will go–totally. So it's not just poverty and malnutrition as such which will be the result, but also the destruction of a cultural identity, of a spiritual dimension of food and so many other things as well." Say no to violence against the earth and yes to sustainable agriculture by supporting the work of Sustain (www.sustainweb.org), which educates the media on sustainable environment. Sustain's campaigns include Agri-Food Network, Organic Action Plan, and Sustainable Food Chains.

Pence and Justice: Spend a penny for peace and get some gender justice. Mary's Pence ("Empowering women in gospel justice") is a Catholic women's organization founded in 1987 that works to liberate marginalized women and to transform society and the Church. To learn about their projects that serve women in need of shelter, education, legal advice, and spiritual or psychological development, visit www.marys pence.org.

Pace the Peace: "For you shall go out in joy, and be led back in peace" (Isaiah 55:12). If you pray for world peace, why not become a peace representative with The World Peace Prayer Society? The World Peace Prayer Society is an interfaith nonprofit dedicated to promoting global peace through the universal message prayer "May peace prevail on earth." With peace representatives in communities from Bangkok to Boston, The World Peace Prayer Society sponsors a range of activities such as the World Peace Prayer Ceremony, the Peace Pole Project, and Peace Pals for kids. For more information visit www.worldpeace.org.

Want Peace?: Work for it. Join thousands of  others worldwide who have answered Pope John Paul II's call for a thousand years of peace at www.pledgepeace .org to create a more peaceful world order. Visitors pledge to spend time each day in some peaceful activity (1,000 years is the approximate equivalent of 8.5 million hours). Some of the pledges listed at the website include "I will pray the rosary every day for peace," "I will keep a candle burning for peace in the window," "I will see God in every person I meet," and "I will pray and live the prayer of St. Francis."

Nix Nukes: Do you have thirty minutes to spare? Use that time to take a stand against the push to develop a new arsenal of tactical nuclear weapons like the Robust Earth Penetrator and the Advanced Nuclear Concepts Initiative. These next generation weapons will start a new nuclear arms race and put the nation at greater risk, say experts. You'll find a sample letter of opposition, at the Friends Committee on National Legislation website (www.fcnl.org), ready to send to your representatives in Congress. While you're there, join the Quaker committee's letter-writing project, which provides background on a different critical social topic each month and provides tools to help you support your views.

Non-Moo Shoes: "The love for all living creatures is the most noble attribute of man," observed Charles Darwin. Nevertheless, millions of animals are cruelly slaughtered each year for food, fur, and leather. You don't have to be a part of this cycle of suffering. Produce good karma: buy shoes, clothes, and accessories made from nonanimal synthetics at VeganEssentials (www.veganessentials.com), MooShoes (www.mooshoes.com), or Alternative Outfitters (www.alternativeoutfitters.com).

Travel for Peace: Go abroad and broaden your social justice sensibilities. Take a Witness for Peace trip (www.witnessfor peace.org) and travel to Latin American countries where you'll work for human rights and meet unforgettable men, women and children. Or sign up for a Global Exchange Reality Tour (www.globalexchange.org) to one of eighteen destinations, including South Africa, Haiti, and Iran, to live and work among the people. Can't leave the country? Look into Sierra Club's Volunteer Vacations. Go to www.sierraclub.org and look under their Sierra Club Outings program.

Haves and Have Nots: Worldwide, 1.2 billion people are underfed. Ironically the same number are overfed. Do your part to right the imbalance. Recycle your leftovers—feed them to wildlife or compost them. One further step? Donate a small part of your income to the Small Planet Fund (http://smallplanetfund.org) which supports the worldwide movement to create sustainable communities and fair economies. Founded by Anna Lappé and Frances Moore Lappé, you can read more about the fund in their book *Hopes End: The Next Diet for a Small Planet.*

Wired against War: Want a womanly way to protest the almost $400 billion budget which the government designates to the Pentagon to make war every year? Work with the women legislators in your state to redirect Pentagon-bound money to the states for social programs. Women Legislators Lobby is a project of Women's Action for New Directions (www.wand.org). Their mission is to empower women to speak out and act out politically against violence and militarism.

The needy shall not always be forgotten, nor the hope of the poor perish forever.

Psalm 9:18

Good Works in the GLOBAL COMMUNITY

Photos against Proliferation: What's the single greatest threat to America and the world's health—medically, environmentally, politically, and morally? Nuclear weapons, nuclear waste, and nuclear power. You can help to create a nuclear-free future by visiting the Nuclear Power Research Institute (www.nuclearpolicy.org). The institute seeks to create a nuclear-free future for today's and tomorrow's children. While you're there check out the blog run by the institute and pick up a copy of the DVD *Nuclear Deception* for only $20.

Water Danger: Think big the next time you have a tall glass of water. H_2O is fast becoming a scarce commodity in a world where one billion people do not have safe drinking water and thirty-one countries are facing water scarcity. Water sources are being rapidly depleted, polluted, and exploited by corporate interests with giant water companies here and abroad profiting from this by privatizing water. Catholic social teaching holds that the earth and humanity must be in partnership for mutual survival and that all gifts of nature, natural resources, and technology must serve the dignity of the person, support the community, and contribute to the common good. This includes water, the most basic of human needs. To join the fight to keep water safe and free for all, visit Public Citizen's Water for All campaign (www.citizen.org/cmep/Water/).

Peace, Not War: "No more war, war never again," urged Pope Paul VI in 1965. But it takes more than words. Instead of watching war in the news, impact the world for peace by visiting Faithful America (www.faithfulamerica.org), an online faith-based community dedicated to building a just and compassionate nation. For more inspiration on peace not war, subscribe to Pax Christi's bi-monthly news magazine *The Catholic Peace Voice* which is free for Pax Christi members (www.paxchristiusa.org).

Just Breathe: You breathe in the pain and suffering of others and breathe out peace and love when you do the Buddhist practice of *tonglen* (sending and taking). Choose a different world, national, or local problem each week as a focus. Hunger, for example: Breathe *in* the suffering of the 36.3 million people in the U.S. who live in households where hunger is no stranger; breathe *out* a prayer for compassion and realization. To learn more about tonglen, read "The Practice of Tonglen" from Shambhala International teacher Pema Chödrön(www .shambhala.org/teachers/pema/tonglen1.php). To learn more about hunger and other social justice issues, visit the Maryknoll Office for Global Concerns (www.maryknoll.org/GLOBAL/ OFFICE/linklist.htm).

Put Your Money Where Your Compassion Is: When was the last time you said "Happy Birthday!" or "Congratulations!" with the gift of a cow, wheelbarrow, or fruit tree? You can give your loved one a gift certificate that really keeps on giving—to a third world brother or sister

Help the poor for the commandment's sake, and in their need do not send them away empty-handed.

Sirach 29:9

through Alternative Gift Market's catalog, *My Shopping List for the World* (www.altgifts.org). Shopping options include Medicine for Refugees in Chad and Sudan ($20 supplies seventy-five children with nutritional supplements for one month), Buy a Computer, Teach Peace in Israel ($12 empowers one elementary student with computer access), or Rescue a Reef in Jamaica ($6 protects one acre of coral reef). Best of all, your donation goes directly to the needy agencies.

Bombs Away: Did you know that there are roughly 36,000 nuclear weapons worldwide, enough to destroy the world several times over? To learn more and to urge the White House to support arms reduction and oppose missile defense schemes, go to the Nuclear Threat Reduction Campaign website (www.nuclearthreatreduction.org). Every minute and every message counts.

Department of Peace: According to Congressman Dennis Kucinich (D-OH), a Department of Peace can help America take the first step toward making war a thing of the past. The proposed bill aims to create a cabinet-level department which would embody a broad-based approach to peaceful nonviolent conflict resolution at both domestic and international levels. It would also create an Office of Peace Education that would work with educators to instruct students in conflict resolution skills. Read more about it at the Department of Peace website (www.thepeacealliance.org).

. . . God anointed Jesus of Nazareth with the Holy Spirit and with power . . . he went about doing good . . . for God was with him.

Acts 10:38

Frances Sheridan Goulart

has written more than 15 books, including *God Has No Religion* (Sorin Books). In addition to the bimonthly column she writes for *Kerux*, the newsletter of Pax Christi Metro New York, her articles have appeared in such publications as *Fellowship in Prayer*, *Focus on the Family*, *Christian Single*, and *Breakaway*. Frances graduated from Hunter College in New York City and now lives in Connecticut.

Books with a World Vision

God Has No Religion
Blending Traditions For Prayer

Frances Sheridan Goulart

Half of all Americans under thirty think the best religion is one that borrows from all religions. This fresh selection of prayers urges you to blend religions, methods, and prayerware (tools used to assist us in prayer). Drawn from sources such as Mother Teresa, The Holy Qur'an, Gandhi, and Native American traditions, each prayer was chosen for its depth and practicality.

ISBN: 1-893732-74-6 / 256 pages / $14.95

Exploring a Great Spiritual Practice Series
Reader-friendly books with a world vision, credible information, practical advice, and easy-to-follow instructions.

Prayer

Richard W. Chilson / John Kirvan, series editor
ISBN: 1-893732-97-5 / 256 pages / $14.95

Meditation

Richard Chilson / John Kirvan, series editor
ISBN: 1-893732-73-8 / 256 pages, illustrated / $13.95

Mother Teresa's Prescription
Finding Happiness and Peace in Service

Paul A. Wright, M.D.

Paul Wright, a highly successful doctor, tells the story of his life-changing, five-year friendship with this saint-in-the-making. The reader encounters Mother Teresa and her prophetic message for a busy modern world through the eyes and memories of an American cardiologist who seemed to have it made.

ISBN 1-59471-072-4 / 128 pages / $9.95

Available at your bookstore, online retailers, or from **ave maria press** at www.avemariapress.com or 1-800-282-1865. Prices and availability subject to change.

Keycode: FØTØ1Ø6ØØØØ